W9-CID-926

THE FUTURE
IS THE BEGINNING

THE FUTURE
IS THE BEGINNING

The Words and Wisdom of Bob Marley

BOB MARLEY

INTRODUCTION BY CEDELLA MARLEY
EDITED BY GERALD HAUSMAN

Harmony Books   New York

BOOKS

Copyright © 2012 by Tuff Gong Books, L.P.

Published in the United States by Harmony Books, an imprint of the
Crown Publishing Group, a division of Random House, Inc., New York.
www.crownpublishing.com

HARMONY BOOKS and colophon are registered trademarks of
Random House, Inc.

Library of Congress Cataloging-in-Publication Data is available upon
request.

ISBN 978-0-385-51883-3
eISBN 978-0-307-95245-5

PRINTED IN THE UNITED STATES OF AMERICA

*Photography credits: Adrian Boot, pp. 16, 34, 54, 64, 68, 72, 90; Dennis
Morris, pp. 24, 38, 40, 44, 48, 70, 82, 86, 88, 92, 102; Neville Garrick,
p. 106; Mariah Fox, photographs of 56 Hope Road; all other photographs
© Fifty-Six Hope Road Music, Ltd.*
*Ethiopian folkloric-drawing representations by Mariah Fox; mixed media
photography adaptations by Mariah Fox, pp. 16, 24, 34, 44, 54, 64, 70, 82,
92, 102*
Jacket design by Michael Nagin
*Jacket photograph by Dennis Morris, © Fifty-six Hope Road Music, LTD;
mixed media photograph adaptation by Mariah Fox*

10 9 8 7 6 5 4 3 2 1

First Edition

CONTENTS

INTRODUCTION

MY FATHER SAID a lot of things to many different people. Usually, when he did an interview, he was speaking for himself, talking to the world, but not needing a question to get started—he was already there.

But he was always there at 56 Hope Road, sometimes sitting, sometimes kicking a soccer ball, sometimes tending to his bees or checking his honey.

There is a swing out back, behind Island House, as it was called then, and my father used to sit with one leg up and do interviews under the shade trees. But often, too, you'd see him lying on the hood of his car, stretched out easy, smiling, talking, answering questions put to him by brethren and sistren.

My father's answers were always direct from the heart under the stars or the moon or straight-spoken in the light of day. Whenever, wherever. He was there, just as you would see him. Just as he was. No dress-up nice-up man doing a thing. But the man who was once a boy from the country town of Nine Mile, the farmer's grandson from the hills of St. Ann who loved his life the same way the bird loves the sky and the fish loves the sea. He was himself a world unto himself. And he said, "Me live in the world but I'm not of the world."

My father did not work for money or fame. He worked for music. "Money," he said, "is like a piece of fat riding the people's heart." He also said, "I have no desire to be a superstar. I just do what God tell me to do. If there's anything me have to do, me a go do it."

His willingness to do what needed to be done was surprising to many people, especially in the 1970s, when superstardom was the catchword of the day and when some artists were famed just for being famous. My father did not see himself that way. Why? Well, as he said himself—"You see me here? The first thing you must know about me is that I always stand for what I stand for. The second thing you must know about yourself listening to me is that words are very tricky."

My father spoke plain and simple words, the least tricky of all. These came from Proverbs in the Bible and also the folk sayings of the people of Jamaica.

He once said, "Jamaica is a university for the whole world; a place where the truth may be revealed." For him it was revealed, and his wisdom comes not only from his songs but from his spoken words. He also said that, in singing, "You don't have no sweet way to sing it. You could almost talk it."

When he spoke, he almost sung it. His words were often phrased like verses. He was wise beyond education, beyond information. The wellspring of what he knew came from the earth, which is why he sometimes referred to himself as a farmer first, a singer second.

Above all, my father was a positive thinker. This was not a response to things. This was the way he was—positive.

He was also a realist. "Babylon must fall," he said. "Is true, so much wickedness must end—but when?"

He gave no answer to the question of time or timing, except to say, "It may take many a year and maybe some bloodshed must be. But righteousness must someday prevail."

He saw the future as the beginning.

Here it is just as he said it on that new day that is always being born today.

—*Cedella Marley*

THIS BOOK BEGAN as a series of visits back in the early eighties when, as a teacher of creative writing, I took my students to the Bob Marley Museum at 56 Hope Road in Kingston. We walked up the stairs to the second floor and there, in the first open room with big windows that fronted Hope Road, were walls and walls, floor to ceiling, full of Bob Marley's spoken words.

For years we studied them, these heartful messages from the mouth of the poet-visionary, the wisdom reasoner, the third world's first superstar. The person who wallpapered the great room of the great house was Neville Garrick, a good friend of Bob Marley's, a visual artist and Rastaman who overstood the importance of dedicating and decorating an entire room with Bob's words.

The words came from newspaper interviews, mainly. Pasted directly on four walls and sealed, the newspapers dated back to the early seventies and, in some cases, the sixties. The typography had a life all its own. But of the thousands who visited the legendary rooms each year, few really read the articles, the clippings, the yellowed and hoary lines of linotype fading in the primal Kingston sun that filtered through the jalousie window slats. The words of the poet had become more a design of face and form than a scholarly path to the wise sayings and prophetic visions of a master. The elbow-to-elbow tourists piled through the museum, yet Bob—alive and talking to them from the walls—was unread by the curiosity seekers who filed through on their way to another room in the house. They looked, but they didn't listen.

The years went by, and one day, my daughter Mariah and I asked Cedella if we might go to the museum and record the clippings, put them on tape, translate the patois, put them into a book. Cedella was immediately for the idea, and so our family went to Kingston and went to work. The tours came through, as usual, and we were spread out on the floor or tiptoeing on a stepladder, transcribing, translating, recording. Mariah took snapshots of every newspaper and magazine article and I tape-recorded the talking walls of 56 Hope Road, and that is how this book began. Seven years later, we have an off-the-cuff Bob Marley book of aphorisms, wisdom, folk sayings, poetry, and straight talk. It may be a small book. But it covers a large geography of Rastafarian reasoning. It's Bob, as he was, as he is, as he will always be, talking personally to you.

—*Gerald Hausman*

BOB TALKING TO
YOU

1

I have always been involved with a hard type of living. My father I never even knew. My mother did domestic work for thirty shillings a week. We had to fight hard. Jamaica a university for the whole world; a place where the truth may be revealed. But money in Jamaica is like a piece of fat riding the people's heart. I don't work for money. I have no desire to be a superstar. I just do what God tell me to do. If there's anything me have to do, me a go do it. Me like meself better when I just sing. More than trying to sing. Singing something real, you don't sing it; you really see it and you mean it. So you don't have no sweet way to sing it. You could almost talk it.

2

The teacher, she say, "Who can talk, talk; who can make anything, make; who can sing, sing!" And me sing. There are those who play music for kicks. I am not the kind of artist who plays for kicks. I do not go out of my way to do another's song. You see, me don't believe in trend or fashion. What people call soul music. To me, soul music is music that talk about truth. It must have a human story to the song relating a real-life situation.

3

very time I play I get that fresh inspiration. So if somebody try to catch up with we, we can leave and change again. Because that's what we been doing over the years. Every time that we make some music, they catch up with we. So we change. Just like ska, rock steady, reggae. If them come too much and call it reggae, we go to nyabinghi music, the first music. That mean death to black and white oppressors. But that type of music, it come from the heart. Every time you hear drums, you hear it. Sometimes soft, sometimes frightening. You get to know it. Like when I first hear Rasta drumming. I think it's something terrible going to do with me. Because it's something that we no understand. And yet it's so near to me and then we get to understand and everything become natural again.

ONE LOV[E]

**BOB MARLEY
& THE WAILERS**
(Appearing courtesy of the
Ethiopian Orthodox Church)

THE INNER CIRCLE

DENNIS BROWN

BERES HAMMOND

**RAS MICHAEL
& THE SONS
OF NEGUS**

PETER TOSH

CULTURE

JUNIOR TUCKER

**LLOYD PARKES
& WE THE PEOPLE**

BIG YOUTH

MC's:
Neville Willoughby
Errol Thompson

IN COMMEMORATION OF THE TWELFTH ANNIVERSARY OF THE VISIT OF H.I.M. HAILE SELA[SSIE]
EMPEROR OF ETHIOPIA TO JAMAICA APRIL 21—23, 1966

NATIONAL
STADIUM

**PR.
2ND.**

Proceeds in aid of the Peace Movement
For further information, call: 927-4579 and 927-4872

[BUSI]NESS SECTION — $2.00   LOVE SECTION — $5.00   PEACE

Rastafari means head creator—God. Mind you, everyone has a different conception of God. He said, "Every knee shall bow and tongue confess, and no stone shall be left unturned." That means whatever your color or race, you will have to confess to His Imperial Majesty, God, Allah. Thank God, we are past the worst. You see, the song comes through inspiration. Then it comes out on paper. But it's someone tell me that. Inspiration come from Jah. It's Jah tell you we past the worst. Is not me tell you we past the worst.

...it is one God make all people

Rasta is all things. Justice, love, peace to all mankind. The God who make I and I, Him create technicolor people and Him make earth and all resources. Yes, pressure is there. And all these things. But which way true? How can you get true? The only truth is Rastafari and commandments that are made by God. Judgment catch you. Because the majority thing that is happening is judgment. A real innocent man, I don't think anything can happen to him. God make a prophecy: those who Him love are those who love Him.

I don't want to write if I don't have no vision. God can give it and he can take it back. Can take you with it, too. I grew up to be a Rastaman. When I wasn't a Rasta, I was only growing. Everyone is searching for something. Maybe all growth is a direction of where you go and find it. But everyone search for it. When I search and find, it was Rasta. Then I notice I was Rasta from ever since. The way of life is what I seek for a long time. Not in the sense of eating and clothes but in the sense of natural spiritual living and togetherness. I never liked the church because they always fighting against one another. So I must find a different way. Or if I can't find that, God no there. So—when I find Rastafari, I say, yes!

God do everything the way Him want to do it. And there's plenty we don't have to understand. The cycles of time. You know, time a change. Because Jah is the greatest chess player in the world. When you have people who think a prejudice way, them take the God out of the world. There is no prejudice. You have right and wrong. The right thing to do is positive. If me hate you, there is something wrong with me. You can't go to Zion, I can't go to Zion that way. I have to love you. Still, I might not do things the same way as you do them. But I have to keep all the hate out of me. Because you can't go to Zion with hate.

ADMIT ONE THIS DATE

RAGGAE SUNSPLASH II

featuring

BOB MARLEY & THE WAILERS

FRI., 8:00 PM

JULY
6
1979

JARRETT PARK
MONTEGO BAY

Globe Ticket Co. — (S) 250

NO REFUNDS OR EXCHANGES

8

don't come down on you with blood and fire, earthquake and lightning, but you must know that within me all of that exist too. . . . You can just imagine if everyone on earth did have one day where we just put all our minds together regardless where the force is, as long as it's positive, and just meditate for even an hour that day. And just live nice with them nice meditation. I mean, now, the climate would be nice, the smog would a leave.

9

After a while I start to think, well, there's work to be done. I must deal with this music God has given me and so this music can carry me. So me say, okay, earthquake can come. But if God send me out, Him never shake no earthquake upon me. So it's not that fate that me a trouble with.

Music
can
carry
you
anywhere

10

Daily, minutely, hourly Rastas pray, you see. Praying is just talk and when you talk, every word you say must be acceptable in front of God.

*Let the word of my mouth and the meditation
of my heart be acceptable.*

So you don't lead a different life and then come to prayer. You make sure you pray continually, so that every word you say, God agree with it. That is prayers. And there's another prayer where you go to some quiet place. And another prayer where your whole heart start praying through your mouth. When you live Rasta, everything must turn to peace and love. Togetherness and helpful: a righteousness.

11

We make the moon and stars shine and the climate get better because people cause everything—God's people do it, mankind. Then we have plenty of wheat and corn. And mankind just cool upon the earth. Me love farming. Me want to live upon a farm later. Me no really want to live in a flat and go to a club every night and come back, then do it again.

If you're in the country at night, when the rain fall it's best, you know. All you hear is the rain play music on the leaves—*rtttt rtttt*. Yeah, that life is sweet. You can tell before the rain, the fowl get excited and oil up them feather.

Pic: DENNIS MORRIS

12

You see me here? The first thing you must know about me is that I always stand for what I stand for. The second thing you must know about yourself listening to me is that words are very tricky. So when you know what me stand for, when me explain a thing to you, you must never try to look upon it in a different way than what me stand for.

The act that 13,000 people celebrated with last week in N.Y.C.

MARLEY ...THE MAGNIFICENT!

BOB MARLEY & THE WAILERS 'NATTY DREAD'

LIVELY UP YOURSELF

13

"Waiting in Vain" . . . nice tune, mon. From long time back. It's for people who never dig the Wailers from long time because they just couldn't relate. So what I do now with a tune like "Waiting in Vain," them might like it, and wonder what a go on.

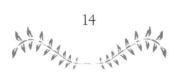

14

really get the recharge from Ethiopia. Because that song "Zimbabwe" come straight from Ethiopia. I write it in a land called Shashamane. So you can say, it's a full recharge. And when the song come out—it just happen. So you can imagine if it was Ethiopia you wrote all your songs, then nearly every song you write would happen. Then, maybe, somebody would say, "Boy, he is a prophet!"

15

They say Second Coming is at hand. The time is coming when everything will be revealed. Rastafari said he'd return in two thousand years. And it's been one thousand, nine hundred and seventy-seven. If Rastafari allows me to, I'll still be alive.

16

y future is in a green part of the earth. Big enough me can roam freely. I don't feel Jamaica gonna be the right place. Need somewhere new. Ethiopia. Adventure. You could start live. I suffered all this our life . . . need some adventure. Africa big enough. Jamaica little small island, you know. When I feel that the job has been done that I and I have been sent to do, I and I pack it up. When I feel satisfied and when Jah tells me that I am finished with this work—it might be the end of the American visit or the English visit—I will know that. When as many people as possible have heard what we have to say.

MARLE

JUNE 12, 1976   15p weekly   USA 75 cents

THE HEAT IS ON!

... MARLEY, king of reggae, is pictured in
the garden of his house in Kingston, Jamaica
where he gave the Melody Maker's remark...
interview on the eve of his British tour,
... opens in London next Tuesday.

Backing his statement that he does not
... success, which would be at odds with his
... beliefs, Marley declared that he
... not see the Wailers lasting for a very long
... he would split from the band "just as soon
... my job has been done and people know
... I have to tell them." When might that be?
"... be any time — maybe at the end of this
... maybe next. Jah (God) tell me when,"...
... told NME editor Ray Coleman.

... ugh an early break-up of the Wailers seems
... in view of the creative peaks they are now
... and the fact that huge American appeal is just
... the corner, Marley and his friends are increasingly
... of their music for propaganda purposes, and
... interview on page 28. Bob talks forcibly about
... as to "redeem" for black people, and his
... passion for the Rastafarian culture, which is increas-
... popularity among young Jamaicans.
... man Vibration," Marley and the Wailers' current
... the most explicit declaration so far of their
... the medium.

... is not sunshine on the isle of reggae. The
... mixed meeting of Art and Business, as record
... and bookers vie for the dollars which the
... will bring, is creating an atmosphere of
... and, surprisingly, there is even a little
... among the locals at Marley's success
... points of view, it is simply envy, while
... Marley's projection as a superstar, and his
... as to "redeem" as reggae's future.
... listeners with a big West Indian population
... thousands of pop fans listening to the
... exciting sound in years, will give Marley
... reception during his concert tour.
... The sun continues to shine, Marley and the
... extra happy — they pulled out of their
... 1974, when it snowed. Marley interpreted
... as "sign from Jah" that he should not be
... new home.

... picture by Dennis Morris.

... 5-page spotlight on reggae, from Jamaica.
... important Marley 1976 British tour—
... strong in funky Kingston" — a general
... the scene in the Jamaican capital. Page 27.
... deal with dark things" — the Marley inter-
...

... reggae sold out?" — an interview with Chris
... head of Island Records, and reggae inno-
... O.

... ng with conviction" — a close-up on
... powerful artist, ex-Wailer Bunny Living-
...

... and the Wailers have been banned from
... religious arts programme Aquarius by the
... on.

... im Marley during his six show series at
... nemearth Odeon between June 15 and 18
... edition of Aquarius on reggae, to be
... e autumn, were scrapped
... ons' Union policy of reciprocal exchange
... reign bands are allowed to play in this
... British bands, in return, appear abroad
... the line at TV engagements. There is little
... unity for British musicians to appear on
... planed Jack Stoddard, MU assistant

PLATTERS   Funk

17

The vampires—most people are negative out there but Rasta people think positive. Most people in Babylon want power. Devil want power. God don't want power. But devil need power, 'cause devil insecure.

18

W e is what we is. We supply the way and prophecy run it. That in this time now, we come to our heritage of culture, our ancient culture on earth. As it was in the beginning, so it shall be in the end. Only thing that can make you survive is to know the truth, and the truth is that God say Him give man everlasting life, which means everliving life.

Me say me life here—this flesh—me have to live. Me never say there was no fear of death, but me no deal with death. Me no have time to risk this flesh too much 'cause it's this me has to do it in. The spirit is stronger than the flesh, which means the flesh is nothing for the spirit to carry. That means there's a way to live—a way, man, it can be done. That's where Rastafari come in. Because everyone else

TITLE _____

AUTHOR _____

YOUR REVIEW _____

NAME _____

PHONE _____

FRIENDS of

*Sponsored by the Friends of
the Euclid Public Library*

LIBRARIES Rock!

Summer Reading

ADULT
PROGRAM

JUNE 4 – JULY 21

Euclid Public Library

preach that when you die, you go to heaven. No, I don't like that one. 'Cause if when I dead, I go to heaven, then where was I before I am? If heaven's the right place (where I was before I am), then I should have stayed there.

A Rastaman

can be

any

nation

19

Sometimes Jah show you things before they happen. That's what happen before them go shoot the place up. Me have a dream where me hear plenty gunshot. And then, the same thing happen. A vision, yeah. That was a lucky thing. Me just stand upon the place. My feelings at the time? Can't tell you. I wasn't even there. There was a struggle. And then me didn't know what happen. But I'll tell you during the time it happen, a real mystic come in. Plenty Jah guide I and protect. The gunmen? Caught? So them say. I know them couldn't shoot the prime minister and just disappear, though. But it's all right. Me don't want them found now.

20

My mother is a spiritual singer, like a gospel singer. I think that is where I hear singing first. Me start sing. Then me write. Me play instrument. I'm a self-taught guitar player. Me don't have a religion. Just a natural thing you're supposed to have. With reggae now you're getting a three-in-one music: a happy rhythm with a sad sound. Good vibration. Earth rhythm. Roots. Me love all music, you know. But rock music really calls for neon lights. Plenty lights. See, a good reggae music now, you could be anywhere. You could be in the hills. I just try to be natural, relying on inspirations. I have many more years of music in me. Many people think reggae music will end soon. But this music is Rasta music, and therefore has no end.

21

Too much people have too much thing to say—and they don't know anything.

22

don't stray from my roots and my roots is God. But I understand that a man can be dead in his flesh, but his spirit still lives. I respect my flesh and I know my spirit, and know what it's like. I don't believe in death in flesh or in spirit. Preservation is the gift of God. The gift of God is life. The wages of sin is death. When a man does wickedness, he's gone out there and dead.

23

Death does not exist for me. I truly know God. He gives me this life. And why should he take it back? Only the devil says that everybody has to die. The only thing that can make you survive is to know the truth. And the truth is that God say Him give man everlasting life, ever-living life.

Inspiration come from vision

deal with one I. Instead of you, it's I. If you go down the street, you see a guy get hurt, you feel it right away . . . know what I mean? That's why me don't like see it. Me feel it. Sometime even more than him, the person who get it. Me personally is a man who is nothing without the inspiration of Jah. God is my father and him grow me just the way his son is supposed to be grown. Him don't give me anything where, when I get it, I can't control it. Me get it just in time, and me grow. The perfect father for me.

AND NOW THE SINGLE

EXODUS

BOB MARLEY & THE

BOB MARLEY

25

M usic can carry you anywhere. So it may as well carry you to heaven—to Zion. Instead of carrying you all about or to some places you don't know. We need positive vibrations. You cannot be ignorant. Can't have prejudice, because we leave our judgment unto Jah. Want to cut the negative thing out entirely. It's what your mouth say keep you alive. It's what your mouth say kill you. And the greatest thing is life. It's a thing where Jah put you through now. Weed out most of the devils. Overcome the devils with a thing called love.

nly Marley is certain of winning radio airplay
new releases, and without airplay it is next to
ble to create an audience. The famous assas-
attempt on Marley last year in Jamaica—in
is life was saved only by his personal manager's
ess to take five of the slugs that were meant for
sician—underscores the problem facing all reg-
sts: should anything happen to Marley, they
deprived not only of an innovator, but of their
ublic figure.

y's international status is currently at a peak.
ring he became the only musician ever to be
the Third World Peace Medal by the United
. The award marked a return to public life in
by Marley, who had vowed not to see foot

that Marley's touring at all, considering the da

The tension in Marley's public life coincides
change in the direction of his music: the new L.P
has little of the overt political content of his pas
exploring love and contentment. Marley's bee
icized for this turn, but as he said in a recent int
"Me write about freedom, not about politics."

Perhaps it's appropriate that at this point in
reer, Marley should finally be appearing in San
after two dates had been cancelled in the p
years. The consensus in the local music comm
that Hector Lizardi, for whom this show will be
independent production before joining the Bill
organization, pulled off a *coup* in getting Marl
Lizardi said, and Lenares confirmed, that Marl

Albums

BOB MARLEY

nding
m only

EY & THE WAILERS: 'Baby-
(Island ISLD 11)

bration'; 'Punky Reggae Party';
tir It Up'; 'Rat Race'; 'Concrete
y Reggae' / 'Lively Up Yourself';
; 'War' — 'No More Trouble' / 'Is
eathen'; 'Jamming'.

ear three thousand people in the
Odeon swaying in unison and
rything's gonna be alright." This
ant optimism that swept Bob
the deprivation of Trenchtown
e auditoriums of the '78 world

er 'No Yourself' from the 'Natty
the 5 'Dread' album still remain
s own the last breaks. Marley has

committed to record. Since
then he has explored
rhythms, looked to Exodus,
and featured with sensitive
love songs; reference
'Kaya'. But never has he
equalled the strength and
youthful confidence he
achieved on the Lyceum
live album.

Bob Marley is no longer
the musician cum poet /
prophet (sic). He may have
been the first on Radio 1
to chant the Rasta mes-
sage when he was stran-
ded in the Kingston 'Con-
crete Jungle'. Now he is
public property. He has a
responsibility to his new
audience and his record
company.

Maybe if Bob had not
survived the assassination
attempt, a martyred poet
would have survived. As it
is Bob Marley is stuck in
the middle of the Atlantic
on board a luxury yacht
with a hole the size of the
Empire Pool in its hull. He

knows it's there and can't
figure out how to plug it.

He struck the ice-berg
'Kaya' and has now
padded it out with 'Baby-
lon By Bus' wadding.

This is a double album,
recorded at unspecified
venues in Paris, Copenha-
gen, London and Amster-
dam, according to the

sleev
note
town
appe
banis
some

Th
produ
like a
cut-o
the b

26

I f you're right, you're right. If you're wrong, you're wrong. If you never knew this, you would never be complete. You would never know good from bad. But it's not only good to know good. It's better to know the both of them—good and bad. That way you can know what is what. You can't go through the world and pretend. Sometimes you must get militant. Load and shoot and defend your right as a people: in the midst of peace and love. Or in a system that is wrong, even if a prison sentence fall on you, we must come together quick. Get it? And that is it.

man is a whole universe in hi

27

I f you want to wear locks it causes you a tribulation. Men not want to give you work. But you know the difference between stepping free and being in jail. Then there are quite a few false Rastas around . . . not every man who wears locks need be a Rastaman. There is many a man who have locks who have a wicked heart, who is a wolf in sheep's clothing. But a Rastaman can be any nation. Even any race. Just so him heart is pure.

I believe we're the children that have seen God. Reggae music deals with natural reality and that's where our force comes from. Rastafari believe in the earth and not earthly mortals.

These are the last days. Everything's going to be all right. Yeah, yeah, mon. Everything's gonna be all

Members of the audience move to the rhythm of Bob Marley's music at the Spectrum last night.

ONE 'LOVE

BOB MARLEY returns to Jamaica for the 'One Love' peace festival. JOHN SHEARLAW reports

Throughout the late sixties and up until January, the year conditions in Kingston had been worsening. Jamaica is an island of some two million inhabitants, of whom nearly half live in the capital city. Unemployment, bad housing and poor wages led to an increase in violence in the Kingston ghetto, which recently led in the declaration of a National Emergency and the imposition of a curfew. "Under every manners ..."

Gun fights and shootings became commonplace, while the Government introduced a Gun Court in 1974 with the threat of indefinite detention for anyone carrying an unlawful firearm.

Bob Marley, shot and injured at his home in Kingston in 1976, was one of the best-known victims — the shooting coming two days before he was due to appear at a rally in support of the People's National Party.

The treaty came "suddenly" in January, with Claudie Massop and Bucky Marshall shaking hands on a borderline street. Since then, on the surface at least, the guns have been quietened.

Shortly afterwards work began on the Peace Concert: Marley's appearance was the subject of negotiations in London earlier this year. "We discussed it with the youth first," said Allsop in Kingston on the eve of the concert. Then we talked with Bob. He accept every move.

"We want the peace to go all over the world y'know. People will have the spirit behind ..."

All members of the Peace Committee were agreed on their aims and objectives and purposes of the ghetto. And the implication of action, committed ... A somewhat unclarified, but apparently genuine, "people's spirit."

We were talking at Island House, the record company offices in uptown Kingston. Marley himself was a mood smiling, red-eyed and skilfully avoiding the attentions of the news posse of "foreign journalists" down in for the concert. "One presence — and the resultant 'best behaviour' of everyone involved in the concert (including the audience) was continuously emphasised.

Massop continued: "Reggae music bring peace, seen? Local artists for local people. The whole movement comes from God, Bob doing it through the power of His Majesty Selassie-I."

"The show is for one-ness, togetherness and unity", he concluded.

Bob Marley, meanwhile, had split for the beach, ...

JAMAICA is the home of reggae and Rastafarianism — the two now inextricably linked. The former, now approaching the island's third biggest industry (behind bauxite and tourism), produces some of the best music in the world. Immediate and innovatory, seen?

The latter has a faith to call originating in Jah. It's members believe that Haile Selassie is the Black Messiah who appeared in the flesh for the redemption of black people exiled in the world of white oppressors. Eventually they believe they will be repatriated, for the moment they live in a land of oppression — Babylon. To many Jamaica is Babylon.

I'm chiefly recognisable by their 'dreadlocks', the red, green and gold colours, and the ritual smoking of large amounts of ganja, the Rastas now appear at all levels in Jamaican society. The last obstacle to acceptance lies with the ganja — still illegal in Jamaica, although it grows in the hills in vast quantities.

"A natural 'erb, it grow like a tree," as Marley points out.

Yet, while Marley and others' adoption of Rastafarianism has granted the movement 'respectability' with the authorities, the movement towards decriminalisa-tion seems likely. Serious ting?

Some estimates now gauge that six out of every 10 Jamaicans belong to are sympathisers in the faith, Rasta — as the most important and indeed first, indigenous culture in Jamaica — has meanwhile begun to carry the banner of social change. This although the musical leaders, and Marley in particular, emphasise their non-political stance.

Which leaves the real situation as hard to understand as a cloud of ganja smoke erupting from a fired-up chalice.

The Government party are committed to radical social change ... slowly. The ghetto dwellers have turned their back on 'Tribal War' for social change quickly. And somewhere in between lies the hopeful unity (Marley's "unity") with reggae, Rastafarianism and discipline.

"One Love." The healing of the nation.

So, as they say, there we were. Plane loads of 'foreign journalists' (distinguished — or otherwise) descending on Kingston for the concert. "You come for Marley?" The constant request. And the real hope? We write nice things about Jamaica ("everything cool then").

And, of course, the constant paradox. "Naddresd no' head dreadlock." Whites are conspicuous in Kingston. For half the (Press) party paranoia ruled. You don't go out of a cab in downtown Kingston at night. Fair enough. One journalist was confronted, in the middle of the day, by three people wielding planks with nails. Other ludicrous stories abounded. "Muggers" were imagined at every corner.

On one visit we strayed on foot from the main market only to be turned back by a police wagon whose occupants warned: "You go back man, you be careful!". Parts of Kingston are dangerous; it's a big city.

Ultraconscious, too, of its own problems. 'Take this from the (left wing) Daily News: "Atop our seething volcano", the story led. "The unrest in downtown Kingston (see above) could be the first rumble of the volcano ... action is needed now to stop the tidal wave that is threatening."

But despite an underlying tenseness the island, and the city, is unique. For a start there's reggae ... and that's enough. Third World emergence, Cuban influence, social upheaval, whatever, you can't take away the music.

CONTINUED PAGE 10

Inside the National Stadium

Left to right: Prim...

right. I mean plenty things can happen, people gone, they don't turn back. It's when you coming forward that you see what you see. Because God no partial. He give you life, he give you freedom. You can hate Him if you want. You can love Him if you want. You can respect Him if you want. You can know Him if you want. You can do anything. You see, God is a very generous man. He give you yourself and then he give you the universe. Everything gonna be all right.

28

You go to church, you come back out, and go to work. Well, me not into that. Religion is a thing that might cause trial and tribulation. I and I . . . not me and you, and them. I and I is one. We must deal with the One. That means if the war is not for the black man, he should then teach the white man the better way. The truth cuts hard, you know. When you kill a guy, the guy just dead. But when you tell him the truth, it hurts for all ten years. Check the children born now. Them born wise. I know that, as a Rastaman: my children grow good. I show them the outside world, and their freedom inside it. I am Rasta; and Rasta is Rasta. I know I born Rasta. I come free and educate myself . . . it take me a long time, even before me start here about a little black history.

really don't come to talk to the big guys, you know. I come to talk to the children who never hear it yet. I mean, say I have to play so that when the big brother buy it and carry it home, the little children have to understand it. I not going to carry it out nowhere the children can't understand, because the children are more important at the moment. So the only thing you can do is educate them. You show the black, the white man, you show the Chinese, all of them. And you on earth, you move in one consciousness. Like, say, some of them think they belong somewhere else from where they are, well, it don't work like that. And check it—all the Black Power and those movement—it don't work. You have to do something harder than that. The people who fight against you, you have to understand why them fight against you. That's why sometimes when I play, you find pure white people there. I must stop calling them people because it's just putting them in a bracket. They are I and I; and I and I. One strong man.

Records

Bob Marley's Survival is essential

Bob Marley and The Wailers: Survival (Island): Bob Marley told me recently, "I no make dis [sic] music [reggae] for fun. It's the music I need to ride the message along, and the message is that our time for revolution is now." Tough words from one who on his last studio album asked "is this love that I'm feeling?"

Marley's current militant fever is not as blatant on his latest release, **Survival**. His anger is subtly disguised by a plaintive, often childlike voice that integrates a purely native sounding music tending to soften potential impact.

On the surface, **Survival** recalls Marley's pensive moody classic of 1977, **Exodus**, not so much in instrumentation but in Marley's condemning yet articulate stab at the capitalist system or "Babylon." Marley's artistic militancy often draws criticism for being harsh or brutal. However, like Bob Dylan, Marley is a

keyboard and guitar rhyth sparkles, especially on "Wake And Live," and the sweet, s sea breeze whisper/scream "Babylon System."

Marley's production tec niques have matured notably a finally present a deft balance words and music. The Waile manipulate moods, unlike p vious albums where a great d of music compromise dominate The band now operates on seve authentic island vibratio Marley's not trying to s anything by you, he's no lon begging for attention.

Numerous ears and feelin will undoubtedly smart fr Survival's frank assessment life during wartime. (Neyeswa

30

That message—"I Shot the Sheriff"—a kind of diplomatic statement. You have to kind of suss things out. "I Shot the Sheriff" is like: I shot wickedness. That's not really a sheriff; it's just the elements of wickedness, you know. How wickedness can happen. . . . People have been judging you, and you can't stand it no more, and you explode. You just explode. So it really carry a message, you know. Clapton asked me about the song because when Clapton finish the song, they didn't know the meaning. . . . Him like the kind of music and him like the melody and then him make "I Shot the Sheriff." I don't know if it's because Elton John say, "Don't shoot me, I'm only the piano player," Bob Dylan say, "Take the badge off me, Ma, I don't want to shoot them anymore," and this one man say, "I shot the sheriff." That song never fit no one else but Eric Clapton.

very song we sing come true, you know. It all happen in real life. Some songs are too early. Some happen immediately. But all of them happen. "Burning and Looting" happen. So much time, it's a shame. The curfew, yes, mon, everything happen. Same thing with "Guiltiness." These are the big fish that always try to eat up the small fish; they would do anything to materialize their every wish. You always have big fish because they manufacture them. That's all. I don't have to sing no more song. Just that one line—"Guiltiness rest on their conscience."

Tell the children the truth

32

Jamaica is a place where you learn to put off things. Nothing is important that much. In America, you got to get it, got to get it! People come from America to Jamaica, and we say please don't run so fast. One young girl tell me say, "God-damn it, one telephone run Jamaica. I live in a house with twenty telephone, and one telephone run Jamaica."

Many people telling me, "Ha! Fool! Your God is dead." Is so foolish. Silly. How can God die, mon? These newspapers don't understand. Or they want to crush my thinking into dust. Is funny, so that's why I wrote "Jah Live." Another song on the new album [*Rastaman Vibration*] is "Crazy Baldhead." You know, we gotta chase those crazy baldheads out of town. The song is about the system and what's

happening down here. For instance, we build the cabin, we plant the corn. We build a tall building in Kingston. Our people slave for this country. Okay? Now today them look at us with askance, yet them eat up all our corn. We build the country, yet we have guys who look at Rasta and say, "Oh, Rasta, they no good." You go down to Kingston Harbour and New Kingston and you'll see.

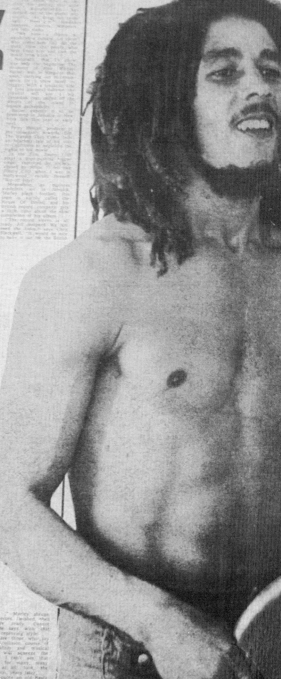

33

People are not taught to be at peace. Education is all wrong. Everyone wants the biggest car, the biggest refrigerator. Crazy, mon.

This is the system I keep talking about. If Castro help Jamaica, Jamaica go socialist. If America help Jamaica, it go capitalist. Suppose if Jamaica go Rasta, no one would be interested.

All the people who say Ethiopia is starving, them could help feed the people. The big nations don't want to give anything without you take capitalism or communism with it. Mankind do that to mankind. Whether from Africa, Russia, or anywhere. Just mankind on the face of the earth.

Man will be kinder to man . . .

LIVELY UP YOURSELF

Idris Walters on the m
the Rasta background
The Wailers.

The Wailers make a p
music. It ties knots in
ates clots in the brain
new set of muscles. B
stampede'. It *belongs*
it *speaks for* a commu

The Rastafarians as
community ranging fr
vincing religiousness t
style to a pithy middle

In a sense we are st
community. At presen
of Rasta music and Ra
happens to sell record
buyers; but as with the
cultural phenomena (
Biriani Indian Classica
The Singing Plumber,
O'Boogie, Hare Hare S
there is danger on the
the Wailers have an im
hang on to. Watch ou
Watch out Batley Var

∗ ∗

Bob Marley and The W
Jamaican rock and rol
Classical JA Music or
finest Jamaican rock a
viscous and the murkie
spectacle, they project
image; they made the
their very own and co
fort with an excellent
Dread, on the Island la

The Wailers have a
and a bag full of recei
the crookedest busines
indulgences. They mig
the mid-Atlantic's grea
since Jimi Hendrix hu
band gear and sold his
industry.

Bob Marley is a goo
Leader of the Pack. He
protects him from the
calypso music that his
him, he comes out of a
ghetto, he's black, he's

The Sardine Lift

Rastafarianism is man
a Revolution, a hip ese
Power sideshow, a fun
world-scale nuance of
source of Music, a goo
Candle down a middle
ecological adventure p
way its commitment ju
eration. Whether a bla
Ex-patriot Ethiopian
Club or just one under
thousands that western
cratic Electronics Inc)
tolerate at its own risk
contributed some rock
kind of chronology:

1565: Queen Elizabet
grants Charter to infan
to sardine-lift Maroon
Africans across the Atl
Jesus of Lubek. Chains
1920s: Marcus Garvey,
evangelist, hustles arou
message that Black Kin
in Africa and that He w
people home again. See
Chapter Five. Convene

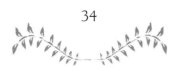

34

As a youth I was always active, never lazy. I learned a trade—welding. So dealing with those things is part of my thing. I enjoy dealing with parts, part work. And I never really mind because I just did it as much as I wanted to do it. Anytime I felt fed up I didn't look for a job. I come from country and country is always good. You grow everything. You don't really have to go out there and kill yourself to get a place or have money. You can eat and bathe and make clothes and build your own house. But in a strange land you can't find a place or settle down. The best way out is to organize and leave.

Bob Marley: In Retrospect

BY PATRICIA SPENCE

Now on the lp "Exodus" his lyricism crystallizes itself in two forms. The first surfaces on the two beautifully simple songs "Waiting In Vain" and "Turn Your Lights Down Low" where Marley is at his sensitive best. The second comes out on "So Much Things To Say" and "Guiltness."

However, whatever's new and different about "Exodus" it certainly reverberates Marley's continued musical growth as well as his eagerness to capture a larger market. (The title track breaks well into the disco medium). Although I still think the best is yet to come and that perhaps another milestone album is on the horizon.

MARLEY'S DREADLOCKS

Although we in the U.S. won't get the opportunity to see Marley perform any of his new material due to his too point in his career. For one thing, he's captured world-wide media attention as a result of that unfortunate shooting incident in his home earlier this year. But more recently he seems to have fallen victim to that same media's manipulation and distortion. It's been reported in the papers that Marley's cut his dreadlocks, significant in only that as a reputed rastafari this would be considered the act of a heretic. Other publications paint him as some sort of "revolutionary lover" reporting he likes music, soccer and women in that order. The press certainly haven't been taking him seriously a factor which may in the long run prove to be undermining. Marley may have to take them seriously to protect himself from such media manipulation if he wants his reputation to remain intact.

LONDON CONCERT

Luckily I had a chance to view a video tape of his London concert staged in May of this year. Frankly I found him in good form. He was his usual self, totally in control slowly building his repertoire of songs to a fever pitch and making it seem so terribly easy. Beginning with an oldie but goodie, "Lively Up Yourself" during which his apparently new American lead guitarist, Junior Marvin, offered some antics of his own, he moved on to the crowd pleaser "No Woman, No Cry" during which he really loosed up and paved the way for the one song that invariably prompts audience participation "Get Up, Stand Up."

35

The game is survival and it's going to be much tougher in the times to come. The Rastaman sees the light of truth and reality, but there are a lot of blind people who haven't seen the light yet. And it's those people the Babylon system has fooled . . . economic pressures, nine-to-five job. Let's say you spend your day in a machine shop. If you stop to think about anything else, your hand get chop off. That's how Babylon control your mind. The system marking you . . . money may be the most important thing in the world for some, but not to me. True, money don't make you suffer; money don't make you don't suffer.

Money is foolishness. I believe the only thing that really matters is for a man to find the way of life and to live according to what he believes. If he does that then everything else he's doing will be good.

We are
the childre
of the Hig
ma

36

My songs have a message of righteousness whether you are black or white. Listen, mon, you know I am no prejudice about myself. Well, me no dip on nobody's side. Me no dip on the black man's side. Nor the white man's side. Me dip 'pon God's side, the man who create me, who cause me to come from black and white, who give me this talent. Prejudice is a chain; it can hold you. If you prejudice you can't move. Never get nowhere with that. I wish things would change without hurt. I wish righteousness would reign forever. Let righteousness cover the earth like the water cover the sea.

37

When me go to Ethiopia, me see some painting in red, gold, and green. It look like it about forty-five years old, the color wash off. And when you go to Jamaica, mon have him red, gold, and green thing same way; so we gwan live, you know, we have our life. Everything that red, green, and gold pass through it look like judgment. Because when this earth fly the red, gold, and green flag all about, you know the judgment pass. During my time when I was a young little Rasta youth, me just try to enjoy myself in Rasta work. When me see anything in red, gold, and green, me check it serious, like it's coming as a message. When me look 'pon the street life, me see that red, gold, and green control the earth. Everywhere you go on earth, the stoplight is red, gold, and green. It's scientific, and it's psychological. You see them stoplights stuck on red, gold, and green. It's a control thing you carry in a memory box.

38

You have to come together by peace. You have to come together by war. . . . We want to come together, and when we come together, them see how strong we are. But as long as we scattered . . . innocent people get hurt. Madness. Them can't come and deal with I and I that way. The judgment will be terrible: mankind killing each other. Them thing now—that is strictly the last thing the devil coulda tried to separate people.

39

M e no gamble, you know, Rasta. Men in Jamaica say me win a racehorse. Me? I, mon, is a saint. My only vice is plenty women. Other than that I am a saint to all those other accusations. His Majesty give me a vision one time. And him say don't gamble, and don't involve yourself in a racehorse business. God, His Majesty, is always right here with me. I born with a purpose, so when I talk about His Majesty, Jah Rastafari, I am living proof. I defend Rastafari. See how them beat down Rasta— no work. Divide and rule. Pressure people to bow down to Babylon. But them can't make me bow. Me conquer Babylon and all its riches.

dealing in the most insidious form of racism there is — 'inverse racism' — and you're an arsehole. Period.

Just zero back to those two opening song quotations and we can start to bring Mr. Bob Marley, and ultimately his concert at the Rainbow last Wednesday, into the picture.

"Exodus", the title song

now — what a hunk of old baloney, ho ho — must be the most openly despised toon you could parade before a selfconsciously hip pair of ears right now. But hold it right there a tic. Let's just take the chorus fully intact, change a couple of references in Ms Mitchell's original to a more JA-orientated bent, add a summer-

Bob Marley sad til ur ra Roskilde (Foto: Sys

Marley har dominerende musikere lanse vende til i 196 Frem/ Sumura associflede bek reggae-rhyme som 'Ska' og Blu Rockes ikke Mi Lofthouse. Marle nu ikke så gr treds, hvore bevæget en form rindelse. Da kontakt med et som der fa plader som Natty Dre 1975 kjord eksplosion til at lik opina i as/da

Festival med Bob Marley

PROGRAMMET AT ...Rockudsættelse- et. Og som- ... at der

at damme har det helt fint. Sma fa år efter han blev udsat for at attentatforsøg forandentlig fordi han dotter det lille negre stat-minister. Mi

Marley er som a- Han ar sammenst skal over

S ROCK REGGAE

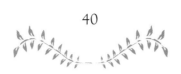

40

What a glorious morning when we land in Liberia shore and behold a time when black man shall weep no more. Behold this big moon just come right over our own land and the big moon just climb on top of the mountain and in your own land, and nobody hunting you down, and you breaking no laws. As it has been said, let it be done. We are the children of the Rastaman.

If me can unite with myself and feel so sweet, you could imagine if all a we unite, how nice it would feel. Jah treat me good. I mon feel righteous . . .

Plenty people read horoscope but all them signs is nothing but Roman gods . . . but when you know is one of the twelve sons of Jacob, then you know yourself as an African. Man is a whole universe in himself.

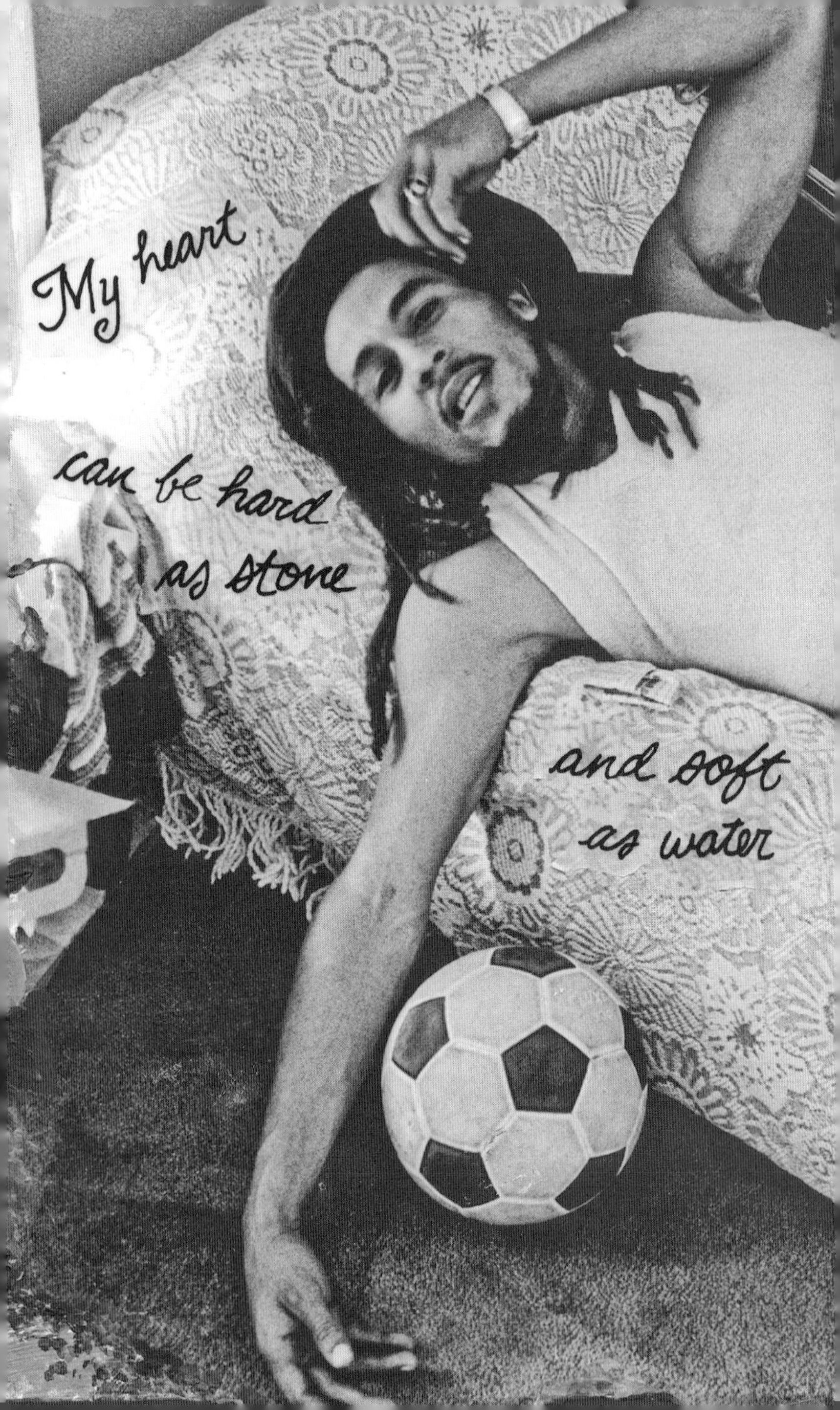
My heart
can be hard
as stone
and soft
as water

41

When I look upon the earth, I see that people don't know them roots. Mankind don't know them roots. When I check with myself, I see that in the last destruction, one man saved, which was Noah. And with him, three sons: Ham, Shem, and Japhet, and them wives. All the people on the earth come from these people and them wives. What is wrong is that mankind figured there is something different. Like it's a different god make some people and a different god make other people. When it is one God make all people. I understand something universal: that all people have one father, which is Noah. Noah was the one who was saved during the time of the floods. So, people all come from one father. So this is the only way them can unite—by knowing them father. Now Ham is the black man. Shem is the man from Asia. Japhet is the white man. But them never come like

one white, one brown, and one black. Them was all black. But man move out into a different climate. Noah give Europe to Japhet; and Europe is cold. Him move out and his skin come clearer and clearer; white people included if them realize them roots is the same. From Japhet we get the blessing of technology. We get the blessing of wisdom from Ham, and from Shem. The division started then—white got Europe, black got Africa, brown got Asia. But if you don't believe in Noah, in the Rastafarian way—you are about doomed.

barn.

Men så är förutsättningarna också alldeles utmärkta:

● **Martin Scorsese**, som regisserat, tillhör ju senare års uppmärksammade nykomlingar genom "Alice bor inte här längre" och "Taxi driver". Men han var också med och gjorde "Woodstock" och "Elvis on tour" — så han vet vad det handlar om.

● **The Band** är inte heller några färskingar. Under de senaste tio, tolv åren har de varit en av de mest betydelsefulla och framgångsrika internationella rockgängen.

De kompade Bob Dylan när han började satsa på rock och elektriskt i mitten av 60-talet, de har gjort ett halvdussin mycket personliga och skickliga album.

Men nu har de tröttnat. Åtminstone på alla turnéer. Samtidigt som de är lite skraja för att sluta som andra storidoler — **Jimi Hendrix, Janis Joplin, Elvis**.

NOSTALGITRIPP

Så efter 16 år på vägarna — från skabbiga syltor till gigantiska arenor — ger de en avskedskonsert där det hela började på Winterland i San Francisco inför 5 000 middagsätande och med ett dussintal rocklegender på scen:

● **Bob Dylan, Muddy Waters, Eric Clapton, Neil Young, Joni Mitchell, Neil Diamond, Ronnie Hawkins, Emmylou Harris, Van Morrison, Dr John, Paul Butterfield, Ringo Starr, Ron Wood.**

Namn som är rena nostalgitrippen för fullvuxna rock-

ry, **Marley**

42

Selassie I say, "Until the philosophy which holds one race superior and another inferior is finally and permanently discredited and abandoned, there shall be no peace." It's not somebody else that come tell me that.

I come to New York, look all about. These places were built long before New York—Big Jerusalem, and all those places. The same architect that built Jerusalem came here and built New York. The same people brought as slaves . . . we want the people to know them things . . . the news don't tell them nothing. The news tell them seventeen guns go off in the Middle East, and there's war. Them don't want to hear about pure corruption and pure killing. They want to know something about the future. My seven-year-old son, him no want to hear about no war in eastern China. We want to hear we going to a level green grass to play.

al moments of everyday life, Wailers and the I-Three are togetherness. They travel school of fish through It seems the idea of family central to their lives — not arrow western sense of the his brethren operate along s of the extended family they always look out for hey give each other a help- mple: Marley, when on the same Greyhound bus that ree and chosen devotees s a dressing room with the and, eats the same food as

teem Marley receives from his people at the moment, Marley was holding down the dance floor, dancing with Diana Ross' sister, Rita. As I watched Marley shake his head and stomp the floor in some way-out Indian war dance, the last words he spoke to Mo and me floated in my head. "We are going to deal with that generation war. Them are going to deal with gun-war. We are going to deal with that generation. This is the generation that seeks God! Them can do nothing for to stop me or hurt my feelings. And me sing any music me want to sing, 'cause me not singing for them. Me know who me sing for. His Majesty the Almighty, mon. It's a war, mon. It's a war. I, mon, a fighter."

SOUTHWEST CONCERTS Presents
BOB MARLEY & THE WAILERS
MUNICIPAL AUDITORIUM

JULY **27** 1 9 7 8

AUSTIN, TEXAS
THURSDAY
8:00 P.M.

Entertainme

the minneapolis star ✲ wednesday, may 3

Reggae singer

43

I n I dream—every Rastaman's dream—I fly home to Ethiopia and leave a Babylon, where the politicians don't let I and I free, and live we own righteous way. That's why I gonna buy land and bring my family back with me. Because Babylon must fall. Is true, so much wickedness must end—but when? Me and I brethren no want to wait no more. Our Jah, him tell us go home to we Ethiopia, and leave a Babylon to perish in it own wickedness. I don't know why but it must be. It take many a year and maybe some bloodshed must be. But righteousness will someday prevail. Everywhere we go—when we play outside Jamaica all over the world, I see a dreadlock brethren everywhere, growing up strong like herb stalks in the field. It gladden my heart to see natty dreadlock everywhere him growing strong. It's future. It be good . . . a beginning. First them grow the dreadlocks, then them soon understand the message and be righteous.